Michael Pryor

Witch Ears

DELTA Publishing

You can listen to *Witch Ears* using the free DELTA Augmented app – you'll also find fun interactive activities!

| Download the free DELTA Augmented app onto your device | Start picture recognition and scan the **contents page** | Download files and use them now or save them for later |

Apple and the Apple logo are trademarks of Apple Inc., registered in the US and other countries. App Store is a service mark of Apple Inc. | Google Play and the Google Play logo are trademarks of Google Inc.

1st edition   1 5 4 3 2 1 | 2026 25 24 23 22

Delta Publishing, 2022
www.deltapublishing.co.uk

© Ernst Klett Sprachen GmbH, Rotebühlstraße 77, 70178 Stuttgart, 2022

Author: Michael Pryor
Editor: Kate Baade

Cover and layout: Andreas Drabarek, Eva Lettenmayer
Illustrations: Anna Knopf, Beehive Illustration
Design: Datagroup int, Timisoara
Cover picture: Anna Knopf, Beehive Illustration
Printing and binding: Plump Druck & Medien GmbH, Rheinbreitbach

Printed in Germany
ISBN 978-3-12-501151-9

Contents

Abbreviations

sb   somebody
sth   something

Photos:
6 123RF.com (Natalia Iashnova), Nidderau; **77** 123RF.com (vanreeell), Nidderau; **78** 123RF.com (Saichol Modepradit), Nidderau; **89** 123RF.com (martialred), Nidderau; **90.1** 123RF.com (rastudio), Nidderau; **90.2** 123RF.com (rastudio), Nidderau; **91** 123RF.com (syuzannam), Nidderau

Before you start

1. Sam, the main character in this story, experiences cyberbullying. What advice can you give her?
   a. when she first receives an abusive comment
   b. what she should do to stop the trolling
   c. what she should expect from her friends

2. Brainstorm words that you associate with social networks. Compare your list with your classmates and group the words into a mind map.

social networks

3. How does online abuse affect people? Briefly describe as many ways as possible.

effects of online bullying

4. Why do some people bully other people online? Write a list of reasons.

reasons for online bullying

5. Read the story. Did Sam do anything you suggested in question 1? Would you change any of your advice after reading the story?

Chapter 1

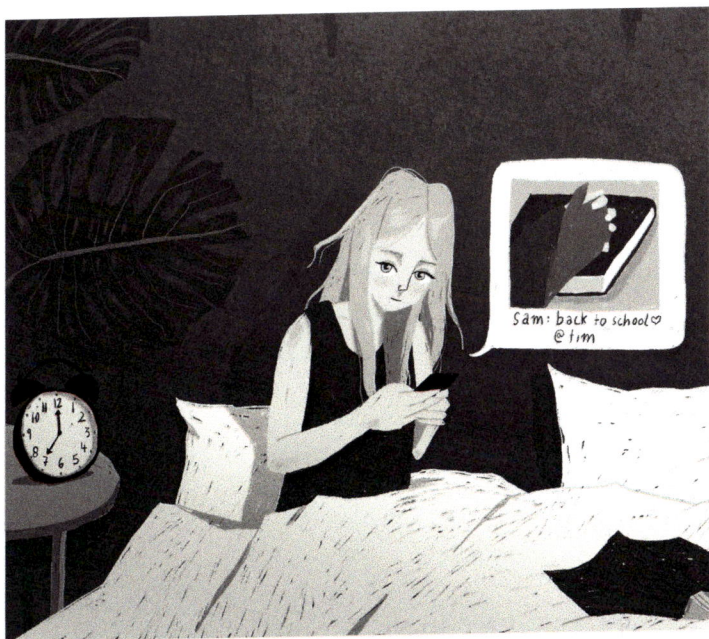

6:30. That dreaded sound. *Ring. Ring. Riiiii-ng.*

Sam threw one hand out and grabbed her phone. Time to get up. Time to get back to that horrible school routine again.

Two months of glorious, alarm-free mornings were officially over.

The first alarm of the new school year brought her back to reality like an ice-cold shower. It was the same feeling every year, but somehow it never got easier.

She checked her notifications, then selected the photo she had been waiting to post since last week. Now was the perfect time. A photo of a boy and a girl holding hands on top of a pile of school books. She added a big heart and the phrase 'Back to school.'

"Done," she said to herself, feeling proud and happy.

---

20 **dreaded** unwanted – 21 **to grab** to take or hold sth suddenly and roughly –
27 **somehow** for some reason – 28 **notification** (here) message

Now, it was time to get dressed. Like a zombie, she stumbled into the bathroom and got ready for school. Of course, nobody *likes* school. But Sam was quietly optimistic and even a little excited about her final year at secondary school.

On the last day of classes last year, Tim had asked Sam if she wanted to be his girlfriend. She was half-expecting it, because they had been going to the cinema and spending every weekend together for weeks before. But just before the long school holidays, Tim finally found the courage and asked her to make it official.

They spent the most amazing summer together. There wasn't a day that they didn't talk or see each other. They didn't exactly *do* anything special. But it was the most special summer she had ever had. And now, they would spend every day together at school.

That's why Sam was excited about going back to school. She would be with Tim all day every day, and everybody would be a little jealous of her boyfriend and their perfect relationship. It was the perfect way to finish secondary school.

Finally, other people would want to be like Sam. They would want to have her life and her boyfriend. She had spent so many years jealous of other people's perfect lives and perfect boyfriends, and now, she would be the girl that the others wanted to be like.

She still didn't really believe it could be true, but she was excited. Very excited.

Unfortunately, this morning Sam's hair was not cooperating. Why does it always happen like this? She spent all summer at home or just in the park, only with Tim, and her hair was perfect every morning. And now, on such an important day, it was a mess. Why? It took her more than twenty minutes to fix it. "It has to be perfect today. It's the first day back at school," she said to herself, fighting with the hairbrush and spray.

---

1 **to stumble** to trip or almost fall, to lose your balance as you walk – 26 **to cooperate** to behave – 30 **mess** dirty or untidy state

She took one last look in the mirror and then at her phone. "See you soon," wrote Tim, replying to her post.

Her stomach felt empty and her heart jumped a beat. She smiled and sent back some emojis, then quickly ran downstairs to the kitchen. She opened the fridge and looked for something for breakfast and lunch, but she wasn't that hungry anyway.

"I put some things for your lunch on the kitchen table," said her mum.

"OK, cool," said Sam. She quickly put the things in her bag and left the house.

Her mum shouted something like "Have a great day!" or "I love you!" to her, but Sam didn't pay too much attention. She didn't have time to stop and chat or think if her mum was sad because she didn't say "thanks" for her lunch. Today was a big day. The start of the best year of her school life.

---

21 **sb's heart jumps a beat** a feeling of nerves or excitement

The short bus journey to school seemed like an eternity. It was only 20 minutes but it felt like more than an hour. It didn't matter though, because Tim was waiting for her.

As soon as she got off the bus, she saw the familiar school sign next to the gate.

Yardley Green School. "They painted the sign over the summer," thought Sam to herself. "It's brighter now. Cool."

And there he was. Tim. In fact, he was the first person she saw when she passed through the school gates. Obviously other people had passed by before, but Sam was only focused on Tim.

She smiled and quickly ran to him. Soon after, her friends Carly and Zoe joined them and they all started laughing, sharing stories of the forgotten summer.

"Well, I hate to interrupt, but it's 8:59. 1 minute to the start of classes. We should go," said Zoe.

"Suppose so," said the rest of them, quietly.

"Don't worry," she continued. "Only 43 days until the next holiday. I counted."

They laughed a little and all slowly walked to the classroom, depressed and already bored with school. Carly had already counted the days to the next holiday. "42 days and counting," she said, feeling very proud of herself.

Suddenly, another horribly familiar sound. The bell rang.

"Was the bell always so loud?" joked Tim.

"Suppose so," said the rest again.

And that was it. Summer was officially over.

---

16 **suppose so** a phrase used to show unwilling agreement

How does Sam feel about the start of this school year?

Why is Sam excited?

Think about it...

How do you feel at the start of a school year?

How do you decide what to post on social media?

Chapter 2

Sam was pleased with the return to school for another reason, too. Her social networks exploded! Every day she received more and more followers and friend requests. She was ... popular! Not Bieber or Ronaldo levels, of course. But now all her posts received a lot more likes and comments than before.

"Wow. Next week, you'll be more popular than Carly," joked Zoe.

"Maybe," said Carly, quietly.

"Of course not! That's impossible," replied Sam quickly.

Of all the girls in their year, Carly had the most followers on every platform.

"Hey, I work hard for my followers," she said. "They follow me for fashion tips, they like my advice and they want to see what I do, hear what I say. It's not easy."

20 **to explode** (here) to be very popular

Carly was right. She spent hours every day choosing the right photo, editing, deciding on a tag, selecting fonts and designs, even planning the best time of day to post. She was an expert.

Zoe and Sam always joked about Carly's Insta-addiction, as they called it, but they were also secretly just a little jealous of all her fame.

So, it was impossible that Sam could have more followers than Carly, right? She smiled to herself and quickly wondered what life would be like as a social media celebrity.

Sam quickly noticed that she was a lot more careful about all her posts nowadays. She took more time choosing the right photo and she even asked Carly for some advice about choosing the best filters. She also made sure that she answered all the comments to all her posts and pics. She felt good, but even though she didn't really want to admit to herself, this was really tiring. And so stressful. Sam was now so worried about attending to all her followers, comments, replies, posts and photos, she almost wished she wasn't so popular. But of course not. It's hard work, like Carly always says. And it felt good to check all her likes and read all the comments.

Sam was in the middle of another boring science class when it happened. Mr Wilson was giving another boring talk about today's lazy generation and how amazing the older generation are.

"We didn't have cell phones when I was at school," he always said. "We talked, face to face. *Real* communication. *Real* people. Not bots and online chats. You should try it some day."

Sam never really understood what Mr Wilson meant. Firstly, she always talks online to *real* people. Secondly, after more than two years of a pandemic, we all had to communicate online anyway. So, what was his problem? "If I'm on my phone, I'm talking to *someone*. A real person. A friend," thought Sam. "And we're probably talking about something a lot more interesting

---

8 **to wonder** to think about – 10 **to notice** to see – 13 **to make sure** to confirm

than science!" she laughed to herself, proud of her funny comment.

"In my class, I only want real students. The only post you need is here, on my whiteboard," he said. "So, no phones around here, please."

But all the students checked their phones, anyway. That was the only good thing about having such a massive science book: you could use it to hide your phone easily.

"Great idea for a video," thought Sam. "School hack 101: the bigger the book, the easier it is to hide your phone in class." Another great idea for a post. This is why people followed her: she posted real, fun content.

Sam felt pleased with herself and started the familiar classroom routine of giving the teacher a serious, interested face, while she was checking her phone.

Tim sent her some snooze and sleep emojis and she started to laugh, but quickly controlled it before Mr Wilson noticed. She turned around and saw Tim, smiling at her. She felt so happy and excited with him in her class. Science wasn't so bad, after all.

Sam was at home, trying to do her homework when it happened. A notification arrived on her phone. Sam clicked on it and opened her post.

"Hahaha! Nice witch ears. You have enough hair. Why don't you use it to cover up those disgusting things? Poor Tim. Why hasn't he dumped you yet?"

"LOL," replied another.

Sam felt suddenly cold as she read the comments. Who? Why?

She checked the username. styloz4real. Then the photo and profile. Just some basic photos and badges. She didn't recognise it. And how did they know she was with Tim? Who was styloz4real? She felt her heart beat faster and louder, her cheeks red as she tried to understand what was happening and why someone would say this to her.

"Oh come on, Sam. You've seen a million times worse on lots of other profiles," she tried to convince herself.

She was right, of course. But this was different, because it was her.

"Just ignore it, who cares?" she told herself. "One stupid comment, don't overreact."

She knew that was the right, sensible way to see things. But it hurt. Why would someone say that? Why would someone make a fake account just to troll me?

None of this made sense to her. Sam spent the rest of the night trying to discover who could be behind styloz4real and why they were doing this.

---

1 **snooze** a light sleep – 9 **disgusting** horrible – 10 **to dump** (informal) to end a romantic relationship with sb – 20 **to convince yourself** to make yourself believe – 24 **to overreact** to respond more emotionally than necessary – 25 **sensible** logical, intelligent, practical

Carly says she works hard for her followers. What does she mean by that?

How do Zoe and Sam feel about Carly's popularity?

Think about it...

Can you imagine life without the internet and your phone? What would you miss the most about not having a phone?

What's the best way of reacting to a negative comment?

Chapter 3

As soon as Sam woke up the next day, she checked her phone, like always. Then, she quickly remembered those messages. She looked carefully at the username again. styloz4real. More messages and more comments.

Now, this post and feed had more comments than many of her other posts.

Sam still couldn't believe it.

"I know," she told herself. "I'll delete the post. End of story. One less follower, but one less hater," she tried to convince herself.

But she didn't want to delete the post. Why should she delete something she posted and liked, just because of some horrible troll?

So, she waited. She checked some of the comments again.

"Witch ears. Be careful! She can probably hear you with those things! HAHAHA!' said one comment. As she was reading them, she touched her ears. Really? Were her ears so horrible? She always thought they were slightly bigger than normal, but not so bad, like in the comments.

She went to the mirror to check. She spent a long time looking from all different angles, experimenting with different hairstyles to cover them.

But it was useless anyway, because Sam's school had lots of strict uniform rules, which also included hair. All girls must wear their hair up in a ponytail at all times, so it was impossible to cover her ears. "Stupid school. Stupid rules," she said to herself, angrily. "Why do they have that rule anyway?" Sam knew it wasn't the school's fault, but she was angry and she needed to direct her anger somewhere.

She searched for tutorials for tips to hide big ears, but it was impossible.

So, she got dressed and left the house. This morning, the walk to the bus stop was very different. Sam felt nervous, ugly, and

---

17 **slightly** a little bit – 27 **fault** responsibility for sth negative

worried. She didn't want to see anyone. What will Tim think of
her big ears? Why didn't he tell her before that she had big ears?
And her friends. Why didn't Carly and Zoe mention her big ears?

She got on the bus slowly, looking down all the time. Finally,
she decided to delete the post. Horrible comments, gone. Likes,
gone. She also blocked styloz4real. Gone. Sam felt a little calmer
now, but she was still worried about all her friends who saw the
post. Plus, the same question remained in her head: who was
styloz4real, anyway?

"Did you see the post?" asked Zoe, the moment Sam entered the
school gates.

"Who is styloz4real, anyway?" asked Carly.

"I don't know. I don't know," shouted Sam at both of them. "I
have no idea. And what have I done to her? Or him. I just don't
know!"

Sam tried to stop the tears. She didn't want to start her day crying.

"Don't worry, Sam. You did the right thing," said Carly, trying to help Sam feel less worried. "Delete the post, block that troll. End of story. Forget about them."

"I know. I did," she replied. "But what if they post more? And why did other people laugh and like those comments? So, does *everyone* think I have witch ears? Is everybody talking about my witch ears when I'm not there?" she asked her friends. Her voice was shaking now. She was angry, worried, nervous and confused.

"No, of course not! Don't be silly!" said Zoe and Carly, together.

"Forget about them," added Carly quickly.

"You're beautiful," continued Zoe.

Suddenly, Sam felt a hand on her shoulder. It was Tim.

"Hey. How are you feeling?" he asked, quietly.

So he saw the post, too. Sam slowly tried to cover her ear with her hand and turned a little. "What's the best angle to hide these horrible ears?" she quickly thought to herself.

"I'm OK," she said. "You?"

"Good," answered Tim. "I'm glad. Look, forget about those trolls. They're just jealous, you know?"

"Yeah, I know," said Sam.

But she wasn't so sure. Now she felt different, without any confidence. "I deleted the post and blocked her," she said.

"Or him," said Carly, quickly. "Who knows? Could be a boy or a girl. Could be some crazy old man from Argentina, Afghanistan or Tokyo. You just don't know."

They all looked at each other and Sam started to imagine who styloz4real was "That's true," she said. "But whoever they are, they're gone now."

The bell rang and they all walked to class.

---

1 **tears** salty liquid that comes out of your eyes when you cry – 21 **jealous** feeling of wanting sth sb else has

"What's first?" asked Zoe, trying to change the subject and distract Sam.

"Geography," answered Tim. "Snooze time!"

"Boring!" they all shouted together, laughing.

5 "The good thing is that we have double sports class and art today, so not so much homework tonight," Zoe said.

"More time to check my posts," thought Sam, as she sat down in geography class.

When Sam arrived home, her mum quickly smiled and gave
10 her a hug.

"How was your day?" she said, smiling. "Fun?"

Sam replied the same, automatic answer she always did. "Fine."

Then she walked upstairs to her room. Her mum asked her something else, but Sam wasn't paying attention and she
15 pretended she couldn't hear her.

She threw her bag down next to her desk and fell onto the bed. She took out her phone to check her messages. While she was scrolling, the same questions came back into her head. How many people saw it? Who else was laughing at her ears? Were
20 they really so horrible? What did Tim think?

Sam felt really tired. Last night she didn't sleep well, thinking about styloz4real and *that* post. After some minutes scrolling, she quickly fell asleep with her phone in her hands.

25

> Why was Sam's walk to the bus stop very different this morning?

30
> Why is Sam crying?

15 **to pretend** to act differently than in reality

Think about it...

Sam's school has rules about uniform and hairstyles. Does your school have similar rules? Do you think they are fair?

Sam watches tutorials for tips. What kind of tutorials do you like watching?

Chapter 4

Although she was very tired, again Sam didn't sleep well.
She woke up in the middle of the night, still thinking about
styloz4real. Witch ears. What was her problem?

Then she made the mistake of checking her phone.

She saw that one of her posts had a lot of activity. "Let's hope it's
not more trolling from styloz4real," she joked to herself, laughing
quietly. Sam felt safer now, because she blocked that hateful troll.

But she was wrong. She started to look at the comments in her
latest photo, and suddenly she saw one with witch emojis. "Nice
ears!" said the comment.

She felt so many emotions running inside her at the same time.
Anger. Frustration. Fear. Confusion. And more anger.

"WHAT IS YOUR PROBLEM??" Sam shouted to her, in her
head. "What have I done to you?"

Why did styloz4real hate Sam so much? She couldn't
understand it.

Suddenly, she looked down at the username on the post.
girlzpower. Another user! Sam had blocked styloz4real after the
first post, but now another user appeared, attacking her. She
threw the phone into her pillow angrily. She didn't know what to
do with herself. Instinctively, she grabbed the phone again.

"I'll simply delete the post, and you as well!" she said, firmly.

But then the temptation quickly ran into her head. So, she
looked at the post. More than 100 comments and likes! Why
should she have to delete her most popular posts, just because of
these trolls? It wasn't fair.

Again, curiosity won and she looked at some of the comments.
That was a big mistake.

"HAHAHA! So true!" said one comment.

"LOL. Witch girl flying with her witch ears and broom," said
another.

---

20 **pillow** rectangular soft bag to support your head when you are sleeping on your
bed – 23 **temptation** desire to do sth usually wrong or not a good idea – 30 **broom** long-
handled brush used to sweep the floor

Sam couldn't stop scrolling. And crying. With every new comment, she touched her ears, trying desperately to push them back, to make them smaller. She knew it was impossible, but she still tried anyway.

And that's how she spent the rest of her night. Four hours until it was time to wake up, just crying and desperately trying to think how she could fix her ears. But it was impossible.

She didn't want to go to school the next day, not even to see Tim.

When her alarm rang, she slowly walked to the bathroom and started to get ready.

Now, she didn't want to look in the mirror. But she had to. She had to try to find a way to cover her ears.

She hated them. She didn't want to say the names of the users, even in her head. She hated their comments. But she also hated herself because it affected her so much.

Why couldn't she just ignore them? Again, Sam tried to convince herself that she was beautiful, that she had a great life, great friends, and a great boyfriend. She forced herself to smile and felt better seeing the happier version of herself in the mirror. And it worked... for about a second.

Then, those comments came back to her. She lost her confidence and her smile quickly disappeared. She heard every comment again and again in her head. They gradually made her more and more upset.

When she finally arrived at school, Carly was the first to meet her.

"Sam, you have to go private. Just forget it. This loser will keep trolling you. You obviously did something to annoy them, and they won't forget it," said Carly, with her arm around Sam. "Trust me. Just forget about it. Social media fame isn't so cool anyway, believe me. Just keep your private account with your best friends. You don't need so many followers anyway."

"I could, I suppose," replied Sam. Her eyes were still red from the sleepless night and the hours of crying. "But why should I? Why should they win? It's not fair. What have I done to them?"

Now, Sam started to feel angry with Carly.

"Why can she still have all her followers and insta-fame, but I can't?" she thought to herself.

And then, a horrible thought entered her mind. What if it was Carly? Maybe she was jealous of her followers. Maybe she didn't want Sam to have more followers than her. After all, Carly was always so proud of all her followers. It all made sense now.

Suddenly, Sam became serious with Carly.

"I don't think so. No way," she said, firmly. "No way."

She pushed Carly's arm from around her shoulders and walked away.

"What did I say?" shouted Carly, confused. "I'm just trying to help you. I don't like to see you suffering like this. That's

8 **gradually** slowly, little by little

what social networks are like! Forget it, it's not worth it!" Carly screamed, across the schoolyard.

But Sam didn't listen to her. How could she trust her? Sam started fighting with those thoughts in her head. Could it be true? Could Carly be styloz4real, or girlzpower? Or both?

Yes. It made sense. Carly was jealous of her boyfriend and her popularity on social networks.

No. Carly was Sam's best friend. Since the first day of primary school. Impossible. Carly would never do that to her.

As she walked off, trying to ignore Carly's voice, Sam felt more alone in her thoughts.

How could she know what to believe and who to trust now?

> Why didn't Sam sleep well?

> Why didn't Sam want to look in the bathroom mirror?

Think about it...

How often do you check your phone? Why do you check?

---

1 **to be worth it** to be good enough to repay the effort – 10 **to walk off** to walk away, to ignore sb or sth

Chapter 5

This was the first time that Sam didn't accept an invitation to spend time with Tim.

She didn't want to go outside. She just wanted to stay at home and do nothing. There was a cool party this weekend, at Joe Walker's house. It was the first major event of the school year and Sam was invited. But with these big witch ears and everybody talking about her behind her back, she couldn't go. She wasn't strong enough for that.

Tim begged her to go to the party with him, but she ignored all his messages. So, he went to her house.

It was a beautiful surprise when she heard her mum shout to her: "Sam! Tim's here. He came to visit you."

Sam was suddenly filled with happiness. "Wow! He really cares about me!" she said to herself, smiling from ear to ear.

---

27 **to beg** to ask sb for sth humbly

"Hey," said Tim, greeting her with a big, warm smile. She immediately felt safe and so important. But at the same time, she felt self-conscious again.

Recently, she was always worried about her appearance when she was around Tim, especially her ears. Suddenly, she was nervous.

She hated the effect that this jealous stranger had on her. It totally changed how she felt with Tim; now she questioned his intentions and feelings towards her. She tried desperately to remind herself that her ears had not magically changed overnight, and that if Tim was happy with her before, then he was happy with her now. The mean online comments didn't affect him, she tried to remind herself.

But her doubts and worries were stronger than the voice of reason.

This is why, against all logic and all her feelings and without any logical explanation – even for Sam – she decided that she didn't want to spend time with him.

"OK. Let's not go to the party," said Tim, desperately trying to convince her to do something except stay at home alone all weekend. "We can go to the cinema. I know you want to see the new –," but Sam didn't let him finish his sentence.

"Thanks, but no. I just want to stay home. Sorry." Sam knew this wasn't exactly true. She didn't have any idea what she wanted to do. She only knew that she didn't want to be with Tim at the moment. She couldn't manage the stress of trying to cover her ears, constantly asking herself what he was thinking.

She hated this feeling. After only a few days, all her confidence, her happiness and her plans had changed completely. Now, she only wanted to stay inside. Alone.

But still, Tim insisted. "That's fine. I'm here now. We can watch another movie from your list.

---

4 **appearance** the way you look – 11 **overnight** very quickly, suddenly – 14 **doubt** feeling of uncertainty – 26 **to manage** to maintain control or influence over sth

Remember -"

Again, Sam interrupted Tim. "Thanks. Really," she said, smiling. I know what you're trying to do, and I appreciate it. I'm fine. I just want to spend some time on my own, that's all."

"OK," accepted Tim, unwillingly. "But, on one condition. You promise me that you'll call me if you change your mind. Promise?" Tim smiled softly at her, and Sam smiled back.

"I promise," she said, softly. "See you Monday."

She gently closed the door and immediately regretted her decision. Why did she say no to all of Tim's kind offers to help her, to support her? She had no idea, which made her angry with herself. Sam started walking upstairs, but after two steps, she stopped and asked herself. Should I go back? Should I open the door and shout to Tim to come back? Like in the movies. I made a mistake. Be with me!

"No," she said to herself, firmly. When Sam made a decision, she rarely changed her mind, even when she knew that it was the wrong choice.

"You're stubborn," her mum always told her. "That's not good. We all make mistakes and we all change our minds. There's nothing wrong with that. It doesn't make you less of a person, Sam," her mum always tried to convince her to be less stubborn and admit her mistakes.

Sam knew that her mum was right, but she didn't like to admit it. So she decided to ignore that quiet voice in her head and convince herself that it was a bad idea to spend the weekend with Tim, even though she knew it was a silly mistake.

"Why did Tim go?" asked Sam's mum, confused and a little worried. "Are you two OK?" she continued.

"Yes, mum. Forget it," answered Sam, angry. She never really understood why she was angry with her mum just because she

5 **unwillingly** not wanting to do sth – 9 **to regret** to feel sad or disappointed about sth that you did – 19 **stubborn** not wanting to change your opinion

worried about her. But there were lots of things about her feelings
that she didn't understand. She knew that her mum would always
be with her, so she didn't try too hard to think about her feelings.

Again, Sam heard a little voice in her head that told her this
was the wrong thing to do to her mum, who loved her so much.

But again, she successfully ignored the voice and started the
long weekend of isolation, alone with her thoughts and sadness.

Maybe during the weekend, she could discover who was doing
this, and why.

> Why didn't Sam go to the party?

> Why didn't she change her mind about being on her own?

Think about it...

Sam is hiding from the world. Do you think she's doing the right thing?

Sam's mum tells her not to be so stubborn. How easy do you think it is to change one of your weaknesses?

---

6 **successfully** in a way that shows the desired result

Chapter 6

For the first time in a long time, Emma felt that she had power. At home, even her younger brother ignored her. He didn't leave her room when she asked, and he always took her things without asking her permission.

An eight-year-old boy didn't respect her. "I don't have to listen to you," he always said. "Nobody listens to what you say."

But now, people *were* paying attention to what she said. People were talking about something that *she* did. And not just a few people. The whole school was starting to talk about Sam's cyber problem. Emma did that. That was power.

She didn't really pay so much attention to exactly what she was doing. She didn't think about anything, really.

It all just started as a stupid, funny comment. In one photo, she saw that the angle of the photo made Sam's ear look a little larger than normal. So, she wrote that silly comment. "No big deal," she told herself. "Just a harmless, funny comment."

In fact, when she first wrote it, she felt bad. She actually wanted to delete it, but she saw that immediately, it got a funny emoji.

"Wow!" she thought. "So it was funny what I wrote. People think *I* am funny."

That's when Emma started to see the effects of her comments in real time. She stayed on the feed and started to see more and more comments. "LOL"; "Hahaha!"; "true!" they said.

Finally, she felt important. Without thinking, she quickly decided to focus on all the people that reacted to her comments, and not on their target, poor Sam. Anyway, Sam had Tim to comfort her. Who did Emma have? No one.

It seems strange, but now, she was just so happy to see that some things she did made so many people laugh, talk and react. Plus, it's only a few harmless words, who cares. Right?

So, she decided to do a little experiment of her own. Not the boring type with pages of laboratory reports and measuring

---

15 **a big deal** sth important, meaningful – 30 **harmless** causing no damage – 32 **to measure** to find out and record the size, length, amount or degree of sth

reactions and quantities like in their tedious science class. This experiment would be *fun*. With results in real time. Plus, no boring reports to do for the teacher afterwards.

Emma started to feel quite excited. She couldn't wait to start. She set a challenge for herself: to try to get 100 likes or comments before Sam deleted the post again.

Imagine that: more than a hundred people laughing at something that *she* said. Nobody ever cared about what she said. Nobody ever listened. But now, everyone was listening, and that made her feel powerful.

She was planning the details during the walk to school on the windy morning. Today, Emma walked faster and more confidently to school.

She was excited about the next comment she wanted to make. She even took some time to contemplate the best time of day for maximum impact.

Of course, she always analysed all online trends when she uploaded her normal posts, but it didn't make any difference. Nobody cared about her. Nobody commented on her profile. She tried so many different tricks. She spent hours on the internet reading and watching videos with tips about how to get more likes and followers. But nothing changed for her. She was still just as unpopular online as she was in real life.

But styloz4real was different. People liked what she did.

"Why do you think they're doing this to Sam?" asked Kelly when she saw Emma arrive at the school entrance. "What do you think she did to them? Maybe she stole Tim from them. Or, she stole their followers. Or she sent them some hate. Or – "

"Or what?" shouted Emma, angrily. "Why are you asking me?"

Kelly took a step back in shock.

"Sorry," she said quietly. "What's up with you today?"

---

1 **tedious** very boring, monotonous

Emma realised that she overreacted. "Nothing," she answered, more quietly now. "I didn't sleep too well last night, I suppose."

She should control herself. Imagine if people discovered that she was Sam's troll. She would lose the few friends she had. She tried to clear her mind and think of something more normal to talk about and distract Kelly.

"Did you see that video about..." she started, but then Kelly hit her on the arm.

"Look! Here comes Sam. She looks really down," said Kelly excitedly. "Do you think she saw those comments and ..."

"I don't know!" shouted Sam. She suddenly realised she was losing control again. "I mean, I suppose. She's always online. Everyone else saw it as well," she continued, quietly again.

"That's true. Poor Sam. She doesn't deserve this," said Kelly, sadly.

They both watched Sam cross the school yard, trying to analyse her emotions, although both girls had very different ideas running through their minds as they observed Sam's slow walk.

That same emotion in Emma's chest returned. She felt excited, powerful and a little nervous. She could almost feel the adrenaline running in her blood. She looked down at her hands. Was she shaking? No, but she grabbed her arms to try to hide it, just in case.

"Stay cool," she said to herself. "Don't let them suspect you. Nobody has any idea."

"Hey, Sam!" waved Kelly. "How's it going?" she shouted, across the schoolyard.

What was she doing? Why was Kelly speaking to her? What if she comes over to us?

---

10 **to look down** to seem sad

Emma's heart was beating faster and louder now.

Suddenly, Sam turned a little and started to walk in their direction. She was coming straight towards them!

What did Emma like about the reactions she was getting?

How does Emma react when she sees Sam?

Think about it...

Her posts make Emma feel powerful. Why do you think that is?

What motivates people to be unkind to others?

Chapter 7

Emma could feel her cheeks turning red as the blood rushed to her face. She desperately tried to think of something else and distract her brain from focusing on not looking guilty, but it didn't work. Instead, she just felt more and more nervous.

She watched Sam walk straight towards her and Kelly. She tried to analyse her and decide if Sam suspected her. She convinced herself that it was impossible for anyone to know it was her. Nobody knew of her other accounts, styloz4real or girlzpower.

Emma just started the account for a joke, another type of experiment. Nothing serious. She just wanted to surf and use the internet without the stress of people analysing all her comments and posts. People were always so critical of everything you did online. Here, with these usernames, she was free. She could say whatever she wanted, post whatever she wanted, comment whatever she wanted. And nobody knew it was her. That was a good thing, she had convinced herself. Probably. So, when Sam blocked styloz4real, it just felt natural to create another profile. girlzpower. Because that's how she felt: powerful.

"How was your holiday?" Kelly asked Sam.

Emma quickly turned and tried to forget about what she was thinking and focus on the conversation. "Stay cool," she told herself.

"Hey," replied Sam, quietly. She looked sad. "Yeah, OK. I guess. You?"

"OK," they both replied, together.

The tension was obvious. They all looked at each other, then around the schoolyard, nervously.

Nobody knew what to say. Emma was desperate for this to end. Kelly was frantically trying to think of something to ease the tension. Sam stood there, expressionless. She didn't know what she wanted. These days, she didn't want to do anything or see anyone.

---

1 **to rush** to move quickly – 3 **guilty** responsible for doing sth wrong – 6 **to suspect sb** to think that sb has done sth – 29 **to ease** to make sth less serious

That's when Kelly asked her stupid question.

"So, who do you think it is?" she said.

"Don't –," Emma said to her, under her breath. She hit Kelly's arm, trying to stop her from continuing. But it was too late. She already said it.

"What?" answered Sam. She seemed a little confused. Then she continued, "I mean, I don't know. I have no idea."

Strangely, Sam felt relief when Kelly opened the topic. She started talking and didn't stop. She suddenly realised that she hadn't really shared her feelings with anyone, especially because she wasn't sure who styloz4real really was. Or girlzpower. She still suspected Carly, so she had decided to not mention any more details about any posts, to see if she could find some evidence to prove that Carly was behind it all.

"What have I ever done to anyone?" she started. The words were more to herself than to Emma and Kelly specifically. "I'm not a horrible person, am I?"

Again, she didn't really expect an answer, but instinctively Kelly tried to comfort her.

"No! Of course not. Forget about that loser. Those losers," she said, quickly.

"No –," started Emma. She suddenly stopped, shocked by Kelly's words. This was when she started to realise what would happen if people discovered it was her. She would lose Kelly. Everybody would think she was a loser. Or worse.

"Keep cool," she tried to convince herself.

Sam continued. "I try to be nice to everyone. I was really happy before this. Me and Tim, we had a great summer. Sometimes I make some stupid comments online, but everyone does, don't they? Do you think they're jealous of me? But why would anyone be jealous of me?" Sam was talking so fast, Kelly and Emma didn't even get a chance to respond to her questions.

---

3 **under your breath** quietly – 23 **to realise** to become aware of or fully understand sth

"Yeah. I mean, no –," Emma didn't know what to say, but she felt so uncomfortable, she just started talking nonsense. She could feel the other two girls looking at her strangely.

"I blocked one of them. But then another one started. Why are they doing this to me? How can I stop it?" asked Sam, crying a little. Her voice was shaking while she spoke.

Emma felt sad for her now. Sam was crying, because of *her*. Because of what *she* did. Suddenly, the power she had felt before, changed to guilt. She didn't like what she had done. Sam was suffering because of her. Again, she felt the blood rushing to her cheeks. They felt hot. She instinctively touched them with the palm of her hand, almost trying to convince herself that her face was red.

That's when Emma decided, in that moment, to stop what she was doing. No more mean comments. She wasn't a horrible person, she was just trying to make some funny jokes. Plus, she didn't want to get caught. She didn't even want to think of her life at school if everyone discovered that it was her. "This will be the end of my cyber-jokes," she told herself, firmly.

She gently touched Sam's shoulder, watching her cry. The guilt hit her, like a hard punch in the face, freezing cold and boiling hot at the same time, causing her cheeks to go even redder. She hung her head in guilt. "Don't worry, Sam. I'm sure they'll stop soon," she said, feeling ashamed of herself.

Why did Sam feel relieved when Kelly opened the topic of who the troll could be?

Why did Sam suspect Carly?

Think about it...

If you are guilty of doing something, how do you try to hide your guilt?

Emma started something that she knows she should have stopped immediately. In reality, how easy do you find it to admit that you are wrong and then change your plan?

---

1 **to get caught** to be discovered – 5 **freezing** very cold – 5 **boiling** very hot – 8 **ashamed** not proud

Chapter 8

"It's someone from school. I *know* it is," Sam said to Zoe and Tim.

Sam arranged a secret meeting with them on Saturday in the park near her house. "I have something important to tell you," she had told them. "Meet me in the park tomorrow."

"Why didn't you tell us by phone?" asked Zoe, looking around the park, confused. "We're not spies, you know."

"Yeah," agreed Tim. "And where's Carly, anyway? Hasn't she arrived yet?"

"She's not coming," said Sam, sharply.

Tim and Zoe looked at each other, equally surprised and confused again. Zoe was also a little scared.

"Sam, what's going on?" she said, trying to comfort her friend. "You don't suspect her, do you?"

"No, of course she doesn't! Don't be silly," said Tim, interrupting her quickly.

Sam was quiet and turned her head. "Well, I can't be so sure now. I mean, ..."

"*What* exactly do you mean?" asked Zoe. She raised her voice now, as the confusion turned to anger.

Tim tried to reassure her. "Sam, you've known Carly since the first day of school. She would never do anything -"

Sam didn't let him finish. She quickly interrupted him. Deep in the back of her head, Sam agreed with them. She didn't know what to think any more. She hated the doubt, the suspicion and fear that followed her around in her thoughts and actions now. But she told herself that she had to be strong, until she could be totally sure who was doing this.

She took a deep breath and closed her eyes. She tried to block out the feelings and shared memories of almost ten years together. "Listen, you both saw how jealous she was of my new fame online, right? You heard her, didn't you?" She tried desperately to convince them (and herself) that Carly – her best friend for nearly ten years – didn't want Sam to be popular.

---

2 **to arrange** to organise

"Well, no, not really," said Tim, nervously.

He could see that Sam was getting more and more angry, so he tried to calm her down. He put his arm around her, softly. But Sam quickly pushed him away. He looked at Zoe, asking for her support to convince Sam that she was wrong.

Soon, Zoe found the words, trying desperately to show her friend the logic. Ten years of friendship. Carly loved social networks, of course. She loved being popular online, of course. But that didn't mean that she didn't want Sam to be popular as well. Sam was wrong and Zoe had to convince her. But Zoe also knew that Sam could be very stubborn when she made decisions. When an idea entered her head, it was almost impossible to make her think differently.

So, she paused, trying to think of the perfect words, to help her friend see the truth, and not make her angry. Here goes...

"Sam, you know how much I care for you. You're my best friend. And Carly too. That's why I know she didn't do this. Trust me." She waited for Sam's reaction, nervously.

However, she quickly discovered that she had failed. Sam's face went red, she pulled her lips and took a step backwards.

"So, I get bullied and now it's *my* fault, is it?" she said, loudly.

Tim and Zoe looked at each other in disbelief.

"No, of course it's not your fault," said Zoe, immediately.

"We didn't say that, Sam. Please –," Tim tried to calm her down. Why couldn't she see that she was overreacting? Again he tried to put his arm around her and comfort her. Again, she pushed him away.

"Listen. I need your help. I need you to believe me and support me. This isn't easy, you know," her voice started to shake, and tears started to fall down her cheeks.

Zoe started crying, too. She hated to see her best friend feeling so much pain. Especially because she didn't deserve it.

"I don't want to go out. I don't want to go to school. I don't want to look at my phone, because I don't know what horrible things everyone is saying about me." She started crying uncontrollably now. "I just want this to end. It's not fair."

She finally accepted a hug from Zoe and fell into her arms. Sam needed to feel that her only best friend and her boyfriend understood her; that they were on her side. She desperately needed to feel their protection.

"We know how you feel. Believe me," Tim said, gently. "But you know deep in your heart that this wasn't Carly. She wouldn't do this to you."

At once, Sam rolled her eyes. "There you go again. On *her* side, not mine. Are you with me, or against me?" Sam's voice was firmer, angrier now.

Zoe quickly tried to calm her down again. "Sam, of course we're with you. We *all* are. But Carly said it herself. This could be anyone, from anywhere..."

"No!" shouted Sam. "It's someone from school. I know it is. Why did they talk about Tim? They're jealous! They're jealous because finally I'm happy and they don't like it. It's just not fair!" Again, she started crying, her whole body shaking from the desperate tears of frustration and impotence.

Quietly, nervously, Tim tried to explain to Sam. "Come on, Sam. Look at the photos. You don't have to be a detective to know that we're together. You see it in all the photos. That doesn't mean it's someone from school. When your profile is public, you never know who's following you. That's what Carly said –"

Immediately, when her name left his mouth, Tim knew it was a big mistake.

"Shut up! Stop defending her!" shouted Sam.

She took a deep breath. "Listen, I need to be alone. You don't believe me and I need your support now, not your attacks."

As Sam walked away, she knew she was wrong. She knew they were right. But she decided not to listen to that quiet voice of

---

20 **impotence** feeling of being useless

reason in her head. "I don't need them," she tried to convince herself. On the long walk back to her house, she felt more alone than ever.

Why is Sam so sure that the troll is somebody from school?

How does Zoe persuade Sam that it can't be Carly?

Think about it...

Sam gets very angry when Zoe asks her to trust her. Why do you think that is?

Chapter 9

The consequences of Carly's online abuse were affecting everyone now. Like a drop of oil absorbed by a piece of paper, or a tiny flame capable of destroying a whole forest of trees in hours, the effects spread through school faster than anyone could expect.

It was now more than a fortnight since Sam had spoken to Carly.

"Zoe, you have to tell me, please," Carly desperately asked her friend for help. "What's going on with Sam? Is she OK? Why won't she talk to me? Does she think *I* did it?"

Carly was suffering the typical awkward position, in the middle of two fighting friends. She spent most of her time passing on messages from one friend to another, trying to give reasons and explanations for things that she didn't even understand herself. She was getting too stressed with all this pressure from both sides.

23 **a fortnight** a period of two weeks – 28 **awkward** causing difficulty, discomfort

"I don't know, don't ask me," she answered, loudly. Her voice expressed the stress and frustration of the situation, like walls closing in on her from all sides. "She's just – "

Zoe stopped herself before she said something she could regret.

That's what she hated about the situation. She had to think about every phrase she said to the other person, to avoid creating more gossip or bigger problems. It had happened many times before: a simple, innocent comment and the other person completely misunderstood the message. After days – or weeks – of silence and anger, the truth appeared. A friend understood one word or even the *tone* of a word differently to the other person, and a massive argument followed. It happened all the time.

So this time, Zoe was desperately trying to avoid making the situation worse between the two ex-best friends.

"Listen, forget it Carly," she said, too tired to make an effort anymore. "Just give her some time. I'm sure she'll calm down. She's really hurt with all this, you know?"

Again, Zoe's plan to end the conversation and avoid any more conflict and stress, didn't work. Carly immediately replied, desperate to understand and help her friend Sam.

"That's exactly why I want to help her," said Carly, her frustration clear for everyone to see. She understood that this was difficult for Zoe, stuck in the middle of both of them. "Don't worry, it's not your fault." Her voice was softer now, less aggressive. "Just tell her I miss her. And it wasn't me, please!"

"I know," said Zoe, softly. "I know."

Although Emma had decided not to post any more, the guilt and nerves followed her around, like a ghostly dark shadow.

With every comment about Sam, the same reaction took control. She was powerless to stop it. Her heart jumped, her cheeks burned red and she lost a breath.

---

23 **stuck in the middle** trapped between two people or conflicting situations –
28 **shadow** dark area in the shape of sth that comes between a light and another surface

"What's wrong?" asked Kelly, all the time. "Something's bothering you. Tell me."

But of course, Emma could never tell Kelly that she was styloz4real, or girlzpower. That would be her death sentence. So now, she had to try desperately to act normal and make sure that nobody discovered her secret.

It was tiring. And Kelly never stopped asking questions about Sam.

"So, who do you think did it, then?" she asked almost every day. "Why do you think they stopped suddenly? Or is it because she went private? Do you think they'll start again? What do you think they'll do next? Do you think they'll start on someone else?"

"I don't know, Kelly. Just stop asking me," answered Emma.

Kelly was worried about her friend. Why had she changed so suddenly? She was always thinking millions of things at a time, so she never stopped asking, or talking about the mystery behind Sam's cyber-bully.

"I hear they were going to track the user's IP," she said, with an air of authority. "They can do that, you know. They can tell you where the user was, the device they used and everything."

"No they can't," replied Emma, instinctively. She started to worry. Could they? That was a scary thought. Again, her face burnt red.

"Hey, why are you never online nowadays?" asked Kelly, apparently changing the subject.

"What do you mean?" said Emma. "Of course I'm online. Not as much as you, but of course I go online," she continued, nervously.

"I suppose you're nervous about this whole Sam thing, right?" asked Kelly, innocently.

---

4 **death sentence** a disastrous result – 19 **to track** to follow, record – 26 **to change the subject** to move the conversation to a different topic

"Me, why? Why should I be –," she stopped herself before her guilt showed itself again. "I mean, yeah. Of course. Suppose we should all be more careful, right?" she continued, nervously.

Emma was so tired of trying to cover up her big mistake. She was sorry now. It wouldn't happen again. Why couldn't everyone just talk about something else?

The solid relationship between Tim and Sam had changed a lot, as well. Tim was so understanding with Sam, and he tried to help her process everything that was happening.

Every day, he told her she was beautiful, that those crazy online trolls were just jealous.

Sam really appreciated his support. She was so lucky to have him, she thought.

But that all changed after he didn't support her about Carly. Why was he on her side?

Immediately, Sam knew that she was wrong and Zoe and Tim were right. But she needed someone to blame, and it made sense that Carly was guilty.

After she left Tim at the park last weekend, things weren't the same. He wanted to help her, he really did. But he knew that he couldn't support her if she was completely wrong about her best friend. Plus, Tim didn't like seeing this more aggressive side of Sam.

Sam was also more distant with Tim now. She desperately wanted to just hug him, accept that she was wrong and explain all her feelings to him. But she couldn't.

And so, her best relationship started to slip away from her.

And all because of this online bully.

---

17 **to blame** to say that sb is responsible for something bad – 27 **to slip away from** to escape

Why does Emma have to think so carefully about everything she says?

Why isn't Emma online as much as she used to be?

Think about it...

Have you ever been in the middle of friends who are fighting? How did you help the situation?

Keeping a secret isn't always easy. What do you find most difficult about it?

Chapter 10

If her friends weren't going to help her, Sam decided that she was going to go to the school directly. They would believe her, certainly. And if not, they would investigate and discover who was doing this, and why. Yes. She decided to tell her group teacher everything.

Sam's group teacher was one of the most intelligent, organised and efficient people she knew. Every time Sam spoke to Miss Hill, she always knew everything about Sam's grades, homework assignments and everything that happened in every class. How did she do it?

But Miss Hill was also extremely kind and friendly. Sometimes it was clear that Miss Hill was having a bad day or was very stressed – completely understandable with some of the students she had to tolerate every class – but she always gave all her students a smile and listened to them.

Again, Sam wondered how she could possibly stay in control with all of this stress every day, and still find the strength and patience to be happy and kind to all her students. Sometimes, Sam woke up in the morning in a bad mood, angry with everybody, for absolutely no reason. She had no idea why, she knew it was wrong, but she couldn't find the strength to do anything about it. And Miss Hill – with all the stress of homework, lesson plans and horribly annoying, rude students – was always happy and respectful. Sam admired her a lot. She hoped that one day, she could be like Miss Hill.

At the moment, the important thing was to tell Miss Hill everything and convince her that Carly did it. She needed her teacher's approval to prove to Tim and Zoe that she was right. She wasn't crazy. Sam decided to not actually think about what would happen if Miss Hill did in fact agree that it was Carly, because she secretly suspected that it wasn't her. Even though she didn't want to admit it to anyone, Sam knew that Carly was her best friend and she would never do that.

But, she also didn't want to accept that if it wasn't Carly, then again she was back at the start and had absolutely no idea who could have done this. And that was a scarier thought than just blaming Carly.

Sam felt cold with fear, nerves and anxiety. What was going to happen?

Making a great effort to hold her head up high and project confidence, she walked firmly to Miss Hill's office. On the inside, the same doubt, nerves and anxiety were running through her head and her heart. Again, she touched her ears: were they extra-pointy today?

When she finally arrived at Miss Hill's office, after negotiating the labyrinth of corridors and stairs of Yardley Green School, her home for the last 4 years, the nerves hit her in the chest and

---

4 **in a bad mood** feeling angry, upset – 9 **to admire sb** to have a lot of respect for sb

stomach simultaneously. Another hot-cold rush of blood to her
face. Another insecure touch of her ears. Was she doing the right
thing? Maybe she should leave.

Suddenly, she heard Miss Hill's voice, calm and friendly. "Hi
Sam, how's it going?"

Immediately, the nerves, anxiety and fear disappeared. She
could feel the tension fly from her shoulders as her body relaxed.
Miss Hill's smile felt like a warm, maternal hug. She felt safe. She
would believe her, she was confident.

Although they only talked for about half an hour (Miss
Hill had another class at 9:45), it felt like weeks of problems,
suspicions, fears and sadness left Sam's head, at least for a few
minutes.

"I know this must be horrible for you," said Miss Hill in her
warm, gentle voice. "Have you spoken to your mum and dad?
They need to know what's happening to you. You know that they
want to help you."

Sam lowered her head, feeling a little ashamed. Deep down
she knew that she should tell her parents. She imagined how sad
her mum would be to discover that Sam was suffering. She didn't
even want to imagine that her mum would feel so much sadder
and disappointed to know that Sam didn't want to share this with
her. Every day she asked her daughter how she was. Every day,
she said the same thing: "You know, you can tell me anything you
want to, don't you? I'm your mum, and I always will be. I love
you."

And every day, Sam replied with the same, automatic answer.
"Yes, mum. I'm fine. I'd tell you if something was wrong, OK?"
She said the words without thinking. This was her life, and she
just didn't feel that her parents would understand everything
about teenagers today. Her dad called them 'social *nets*', because
they trapped you like a poor, helpless fish in a fisherman's net, he

---

1 **simultaneously** at the same time – 8 **maternal** like a mother – 12 **suspicion** thought
that sb has done sth – 32 **helpless** unable to defend yourself without help

said. "Yes, Miss Hill. You're right. I know," said Sam, quietly. "I'll tell them, soon."

Miss Hill smiled. "Thank you," she said. "It's the right thing to do, and they deserve to know."

Sam felt safer now. Miss Hill's attention and her genuine interest in Sam's wellbeing made her feel calm.

"You know, I've already spoken to Carly," she said.

Sam looked up, surprised. Why? What did she say? What happened? Did she confess? What did she say about her? Millions of thoughts invaded Sam's head, all at once.

Miss Hill continued. "She came to see me, a couple of weeks ago. She was really worried – she still is. About you. She was crying. She came to ask me for help..."

"Ha! So you did it, then!" thought Sam.

"She wanted me to help you find who did this. She told me the same as you," Miss Hill said, quietly but firmly now.

Sam was in shock, intrigued. She desperately wanted to know what Miss Hill thought about the whole situation.

"You know Carly didn't do it, don't you?" Miss Hill's words were strong, but soft.

Sam understood Miss Hill's intention. She wanted Sam to feel that she knew she was suffering and frustrated, but also that it was important for her to accept something very important. The answer to process this whole situation was not to find an easy answer and blame a friend. The situation was more complicated and Sam needed her friends around her.

"I think I know," Sam said, accepting what Tim and Zoe were saying all the time.

"You need your friends around you," continued Miss Hill. "So, go and get them."

Sam knew that Miss Hill was right, but she didn't like to accept it.

---

6 **wellbeing** the state of being comfortable, healthy or happy – 9 **to confess** to admit responsibility for a crime or doing sth wrong – 17 **intrigued** curious about sth

"You're right, Miss Hill. Thanks." Sam's words were sincere and full of appreciation.

With a deep breath, Sam decided that she would have to speak to Carly. It wouldn't be easy to accept that she was wrong, but it was necessary.

"I want to see you both together in class next week, agreed?" said Miss Hill, strongly but with her warm, friendly smile. "That's your homework for this week."

"Agreed," said Sam.

This was the most difficult homework Miss Hill had given her, but also the most important.

Why does Sam decide to go and talk to Miss Hill?

Why doesn't she want to accept that the troll isn't Carly?

Think about it...

If you have a problem, who do you talk to?

How much does it depend on what the problem is?

Chapter 11

It had been more than two weeks since Sam received the last comment. She took the difficult decision a day later to delete her public account and go private.

"Goodbye, popularity," Sam said sadly, as she deleted the account. "And thanks, internet troll. Thanks for destroying my happiness." She was angry that this was the only solution.

However, since that day she was definitely a little less worried every time she took her phone.

She was definitely less worried, that was true. But, she was also still so angry and frustrated that *this* was the only solution.

Thanks to some anonymous, jealous, hateful online troll, she couldn't be famous and popular online. But others could.

Even today – ready to talk to Carly and try to build back her friendship – Sam felt jealous of her friend's internet fame. It made her stop and think: maybe the jealousy that Sam told Tim and Zoe that Carly felt towards her, was actually her own jealousy of Carly?

She didn't have time to analyse those feelings too much. It was time to ask her best friend for forgiveness.

Immediately, Sam felt more relaxed when she saw Carly, waiting for her in the café. Suddenly, the years of friendship, laughs and tears together smashed into her and embraced her like a warm breeze. At once, they grabbed those feelings of doubt and anger she felt to Carly and threw them far away, into a forgotten past. This was her best friend, Carly.

Carly was slowly drinking her hot cappuccino when she saw Sam. She immediately jumped up from the table, with a smile and a wave, spilling some of the hot coffee on the table and her blouse. But Sam didn't care. She was so happy to see her friend again.

---

20 **foregiveness** not feeling angry with sb about sth they did in the past – 24 **breeze** light wind – 29 **to spill** to unintentionally cause a liquid to flow over and out of its container

Sam smiled as well. Then, she noticed another cup at the table.
Anxiety ran into her head again. Who was here? Who did she
invite? Why? What was her plan?

Fortunately, Carly spoke before Carly's paranoia took control.
"I bought you a cappuccino. Your favourite," she said, softly.

And just like that, Sam realised once again how important
her friends were. And how wrong she was to listen to all those
negative noises in her head. "I'm going to learn to pay more
attention to my friends' voices," she promised herself. "They know
me better than myself, sometimes. And they know what's best
for me." Sam was happy with her new decision and confidently
walked to the table to give Carly a massive hug.

They talked for most of the morning. They cried, laughed and
hugged each other.

"Listen, I talked to Miss Hill," said Carly.

"Me too," added Sam.

Carly continued, "And she gave me some horrible homework." But she was smiling as she said it.

"What?" asked Sam, curiously. "Tell me!"

"Well, she told me my homework was to talk to you. She wants to see the two of us together in her class next week."

Sam laughed so hard she almost hit her head on the wall behind her. "She said exactly the same thing to me!" she laughed.

The two girls hugged each other again.

"Well, at least that's one piece of homework I've finished already this weekend," joked Carly. "I normally don't do anything before Sunday afternoon!"

They both laughed again. "Thanks," said Sam.

"Thanks for what? I was worried about you. You're my best friend. Zoe and Tim didn't really know what was going on. They're worried about you too, you know." Carly wanted to take this chance to convince Sam to fix things with them as well.

"I know," said Carly. "I don't know what Tim thinks of me now. He was so lovely and supportive, and I just pushed him away. It was silly of me, I know. I just ..."

"Don't worry," interrupted Carly. She knew her friend and she knew what she was thinking, so she wanted to make her feel at ease. "Trust me: he understands. Well, *understand* is maybe not the best word, because even you don't really understand everything you do sometimes, but that's part of being a teenager."

They both smiled at each other. "He really cares for you and he misses you, too," she continued.

"We all do."

Carly's words pushed two more tears slowly down Sam's cheeks. She tried to hide them with a smile. "Me too," she said.

"Anyway, Miss Hill told me that at school they can't do anything," she explained. "You know they're not allowed to see our phones or our social networks, remember. Anyway, she told me that everything that happens with social networks and on our

21 **to feel at ease** to feel comfortable, relaxed

private phone outside school is not related to school, and there's nothing that they can do about it. Legally speaking."

Carly's words hit Sam hard, but she knew it was true anyway. Just another thing she hadn't wanted to accept before. "I know," she said. "Our social networks are our responsibility. Our life continues outside of school, 24/7. Social networks are another part of our lives. So, we must ask safely and responsibly and listen to the advice they give us at school," she said, copying Mr Gardner's words.

"Exactly," agreed Carly.

Mr Gardner was the school headmaster and his messages were always so boring. None of the students paid much attention when he was speaking, but now Sam realised how true his words were.

"So, I'll never discover who did it, then. Because school can't help me. I'm on my own," said Sam, sadly.

"You're never on your own," interrupted Carly, quickly and firmly. "You never have been. And you never will be."

> Why did Sam decide to delete her public account?

> How did the meeting with Sam and Carly go?

Think about it...

How easy do you find it to forgive people? What makes it difficult?

Sam agrees with Carly that social networks are our responsibility. Do you agree with this? What are the best ways of managing them responsibly?

10 **headmaster** principal, person in charge of a school

Chapter 12

The weeks had passed at Yardley Green School and this extra time had given everyone an opportunity to process what had happened.

Sam now felt that she had overreacted about those comments. She also felt lucky that she had discovered the stressful pressures of anonymous comments online by using a public profile before something more severe could occur.

She made the difficult decision to not open her old public account again. Of course, she really missed the popularity and fame, and the sense of importance that it gave her. She loved thinking that many people would like her posts and that she made them laugh.

But, even though the negative posts were very uncommon, they affected her more than one hundred likes or positive messages. She definitely didn't miss the feeling of vulnerability and the anxiety she felt before and after every post. Would they like it? What would they say?

She knew that it was impossible to please everyone, but even the most insignificant, irrelevant comments really hurt her. For example, she still always worried about her ears every time she brushed her hair or looked in the mirror. Despite all of Tim's efforts to convince her and her friends' constant advice, they could never convince her to stop thinking about those comments. Her self-confidence was permanently damaged and she was still angry at those anonymous bullies for making her feel that way. It wasn't fair.

However, Sam did generally pay a lot more attention to her loved ones and gave less importance to meaningless comments made from others or distant acquaintances online.

Her social networks were smaller and more limited now. This also gave her some more time to spend on homework, and her

---

19 **irrelevant** not connected with sth – 24 **permanently** for ever – 29 **acquaintance** sb you know, but not a close friend

parents and teachers were happier with her better grades at
school.

Sam also discovered that now she really thought about
what she wrote in other people's posts, too. She had never said
anything so horrible like styloz4real or girlzpower did to her, but
she was pleased that now she tried to make sure that there was
nothing negative at all in anything she wrote online. "If it's not
positive, don't say it," was her philosophy now. It was, of course,
very easy to sometimes write things online which she didn't
actually feel, because typing words is much easier than saying
them to a person's face.

"Maybe that's what happened to those users," she thought to
herself. She tried to be as forgiving as possible, but the effects of
how they made her feel were still too present.

Sam was also a little closer to her parents now. Finally, Carly
had convinced her to tell them everything. She even went with
Sam for moral support.

Her mum cried a lot and Sam did, too. She felt very bad for excluding her mum so much, especially because she knew how desperately her mum wanted to be a part of her life.

Sam promised them – and herself – that she would try to express herself more and tell them if she had a problem, although she knew there were still many things that she simply didn't want to discuss so much with her mum and dad.

Emma still constantly felt guilty about what she had done. The good thing is that now Kelly wasn't talking about it all the time, but every time Sam passed in the school, Emma felt her face burning red as the guilt and nerves returned to attack her again.

Kelly was convinced that the troll disappeared after Sam went private and closed down her public account. Sometimes, Emma almost felt like telling her that she had already decided to stop the comments even before Sam closed her account; that it was Emma's decision to delete her anonymous user, not Sam who blocked her account that stopped everything. She didn't though, of course.

One day, Sam, Emma and Carly sat on the table behind Emma and Kelly in the cafeteria. Emma immediately blocked out Kelly's conversation as she tried to focus on what the girls at the other table were saying. They were still talking about styloz4real and girlzpower!

"I know I'll find out who did it, one day," said Sam, firmly. She sounded very convinced.

Once again, Emma felt cold with fear. She tried desperately to look normal while millions of questions and possibilities invaded her brain again. That's when she accidentally spilled her bottle of water on the table, wetting Kelly's sandwich.

"Careful!" she shouted. "What are you thinking?"

"Sorry," replied Emma, instinctively, as she tried to dry the water without attracting more attention to herself.

---

14 **to feel like doing sth** to want to do sth – 27 **to invade** to enter uninvited

"Could she still discover me?" Emma asked herself, nervously. "They say that everything you do online stays there, forever. So, could she?"

She didn't have the answers to her own questions, but her doubts in her head were busy at work. The shadow of Emma's foolish posts would still follow her around for a long time.

> What is the disadvantage for Sam of not reopening her public account?

> Why does Sam think it is easier for people to be more unkind on the internet than in person?

Think about it...

How seriously should you take comments that trolls make?

Do you think it is possible to completely ignore them?

---

6 **foolish** without good sense or judgement

Activities

Focus on the story

1. Are the sentences True or False?
Tick the correct box.

		True	False
1.	Sam travels to school by bus.	☐	☐
2.	As Sam starts getting more followers, she changes how and what she posts online.	☐	☐
3.	Tim and Sam don't use their phones in class.	☐	☐
4.	Students at Yardley Green School can wear any clothes they like.	☐	☐
5.	At first, Sam doesn't want to delete the posts that got abuse.	☐	☐
6.	After the 'witch ears' comments, Sam always tries to cover her ears now.	☐	☐
7.	Tim went to Sam's house because he didn't want her to go to the party with him.	☐	☐
8.	Emma's brother is older than her.	☐	☐
9.	Kelly is glad that Sam is receiving online abuse.	☐	☐
10.	Emma bought a new phone to create the girlzpower profile.	☐	☐
11.	When Emma saw Sam's suffering face to face, she decided to delete her anonymous accounts.	☐	☐
12.	Tim and Zoe agree with Sam that Carly is the troll.	☐	☐
13.	Kelly suspects that Emma is the troll.	☐	☐
14.	Carly spoke to Miss Hill before Sam did.	☐	☐
15.	Carly and Sam both did the 'homework' that Miss Hill gave them.	☐	☐

2. What happened when?

Put the events in the correct order. Write the number in the correct box below.

a Sam and Carly rebuild their friendship.   1 ....

b Emma creates the girlzpower profile.   2 ....

c Sam decides to delete her public profile and go
   private.   3 ....

d Sam meets with Miss Hill.   4 ....

e The summer holidays start.   5 ....

f Sam suspects Carly is the troll.   6 ....

g Tim and Sam are officially boyfriend and girlfriend.   7 ....

h Sam receives the first 'witch ears' comment.   8 ....

i Sam tells her parents about the troll.   9 ....

j Sam's online popularity grows.   10 ....

3. What did they look like?

Use the options below to write the name of the place where each event happened.

Some of the places are repeated.

the schoolyard	the café	the park
Sam's bedroom	Miss Hill's office	the school cafeteria

1   Tim meets Sam for the first time after the
    school holidays.   ....

2   Sam receives the first 'witch ears'
    comment.   ....

3   Zoe, Tim and Carly ask Sam about the first
    'witch ears' comment.   ....

4   Sam receives the first comment from
    girlzpower.   ....

5   Emma, Kelly and Sam discuss the troll's
    identity.   ....

6   Sam asks Tim and Zoe for help against
    Carly.   ....

7   Sam finally accepts that Carly is not the troll.   ....

8   Sam receives some difficult 'homework'.   ....

9   Sam and Carly reconcile and rebuild their
    friendship.   ....

10 Emma nervously spills her drink when she
    hears Sam promise to discover the troll's
    identity.   ....

4. How did you like it?

Reflect in the story and complete the review form.

What I liked

1.

2.

3.

What I didn't like

1.

2.

3.

My favourite character is _____ because:

My favourite chapter is _____ because:

Stars: _____ / 5

Focus on the people

1. Sam

How would you describe Sam?
Choose 5 adjectives to describe her and
give reasons or examples from the text.

Sam is …

adjective	reason / example
a	
b	
c	
d	
e	

2. Who did what?

Read the sentences and decide which character did what.

Miss Hill	Sam	styloz4real	Emma	Kelly
Mr Wilson	Tim	Sam's mum	Zoe	Carly

1 .... is Sam's insta-addict friend, an online celebrity.
2. .... thinks that the young generation are lazy.
3. .... is the first online profile that starts to bully Sam.
4. .... always asks Sam how her day is, but rarely receives a reply from Sam.
5 .... is a friendly, happy and caring person who convinces Sam that Carly is not the troll.
6. .... deletes her popular public accounts and misses the popularity, but not the vulnerability of social media fame.
7. .... asked Sam to be his girlfriend at the end of the last school year.
8. .... is very curious and is always asking and thinking millions of things at once; wants to know who the troll is.
9. .... is 'stuck in the middle' between Sam and Carly when Sam decides to ignore Carly.
10. .... constantly feels guilty for the hurtful comments she made online.

Focus on grammar

1. Adjective or noun?

Look at some or the emotions and feelings that Sam and Emma experience during the story.

Complete the table with the corresponding noun or adjective form. Use a dictionary to help you if necessary.

adjective		noun		adjective		noun
anxious	-			optimistic	-	
	-	anger		paranoid	-	
	-	confidence		popular	-	
confused	-			powerful	-	
	-	doubtful			-	relief
	-	excitement		sad	-	
	–	fearful			-	safety
frustrated	-				-	self-consciousness
	-	guilt		stressed	-	
happy	-			surprised	-	
important	-				-	suspicion
jealous	-				-	tension
	-	loneliness		ugly	-	
lucky	-				-	vulnerability
	-	nerves		worried	-	

2. Forming questions

Questions are sometimes hard to organise. Put the words in the correct order to form questions from the story.

1 yet / he / you / hasn't / dumped / why / ?

....

2 someone / that / why / would / say / ?

....

3 have / that / why / they / do / rule / ?

....

4 her / ears / Tim / will / what / of / big / think / ?

....

5 Carly / didn't / mention / ears / and / Zoe / why / big / her / ?

....

6 her / I / done / to / have / what / ?

....

7 everyone / think / does / have / witch / I / ears / ?

....

8 me / why / they / to / doing / are / this / ?

....

9 why / you / by / didn't / us / phone / tell / ?

....

10 everyone / just / else / why / about / something / talk / couldn't / ?

....

3. Past perfect or past simple?

We use the past perfect to describe an action that happened *before* another action point in the past.

Look at these sentences from the story. Circle the action that *happens first, before* the other action.

1 Sam <u>had blocked</u> styloz4real, but another user <u>appeared</u>.

2 Sam <u>realised</u> that she <u>hadn't shared</u> her feelings with anyone.

3 Suddenly, the power that Emma <u>had felt</u> before, <u>changed</u> to guilt.

4 Carly quickly <u>discovered</u> that she <u>had failed</u>.

5 It <u>had happened</u> many times before: a simple, innocent comment and the other person completely <u>misunderstood</u> the message.

6 Although Emma <u>had decided</u> not to post any more, the guilt and nerves <u>followed</u> her around, like a ghostly dark shadow.

7 Sam now <u>felt</u> that she <u>had overreacted</u> about those comments.

8 Emma still constantly <u>felt</u> guilty about what she <u>had done</u>.

9 Emma <u>had already decided</u> to stop the comments even before Sam <u>closed</u> her account.

Build your vocabulary

Focus on words

1. Emotions and feelings

All of the characters experience a range of emotions and feelings during the story, especially Sam and Emma.

Complete the circles with the emotions and feelings that Sam and Emma experience.

Emma's emotions and feelings

bad	excited	fear	guilty	important
	nervous	powerful	sad	

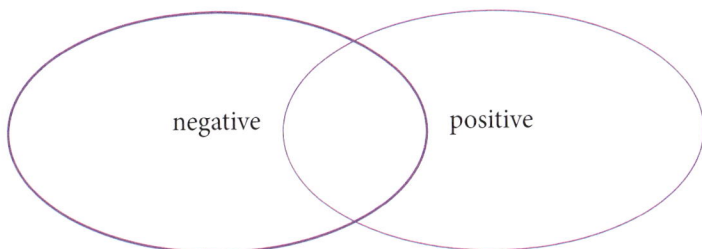

negative   positive

Sam's emotions and feelings

alone	anger	anxiety	confident	confused
doubt	excited	fear	frustrated	happy
jealous	lucky	nervous	optimistic	paranoid
pleased	popular	relaxed	relief	safe
scared	self-conscious	stressed	surprised	suspicious
tense	ugly	upset	vulnerable	worried

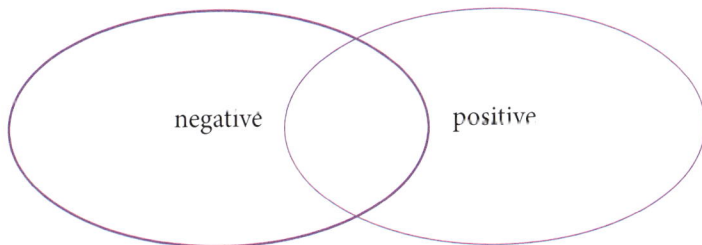

negative   positive

Witch Ears – the mind map

Expand the mind map with words from the story and other words you know.

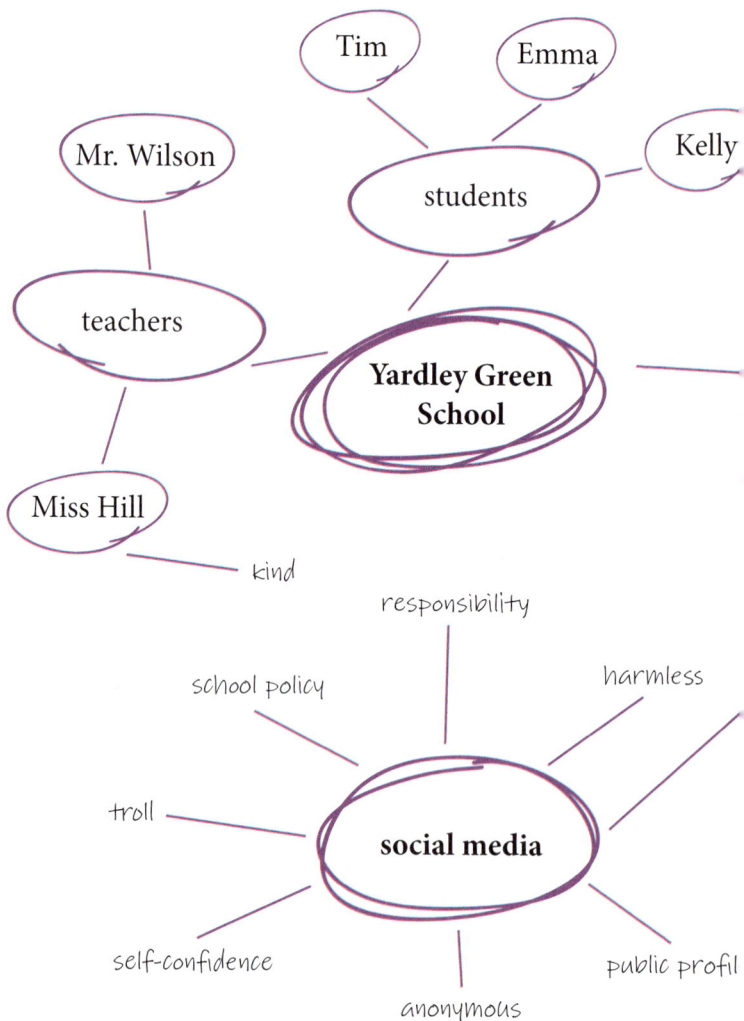

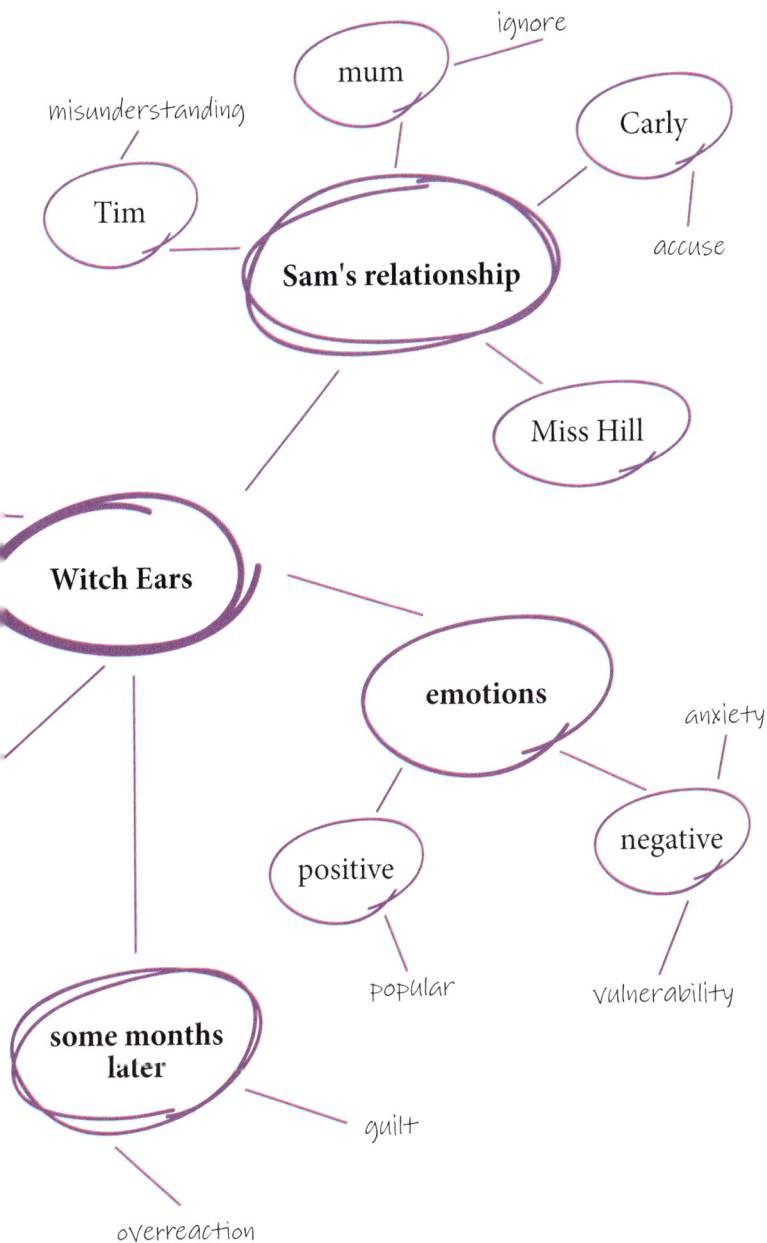

ignore

mum

Carly

misunderstanding

accuse

Tim

Sam's relationship

Miss Hill

Witch Ears

emotions

anxiety

negative

positive

popular

vulnerability

some months later

guilt

overreaction

Glossary

	New word?	Notes / connected words

relationships

acquaintance	☐
advice	☐
approval	☐
argument	☐
authority	☐
favour	☐
genuine	☐
intention	☐
mistake	☐
patience	☐
protection	☐
sincere	☐
supportive	☐
tear	☐
thought	☐
wellbeing	☐

relationships - verbs

admire	☐
agree	☐
appreciate	☐
beg	☐
believe	☐
calm down	☐
comfort	☐
confess	☐
convince	☐
defend	☐
dump	☐
fight	☐

	New word?	Notes / connected words
greet	☐	
hug	☐	
joke	☐	
laugh	☐	
pretend	☐	
respect	☐	
smile	☐	
support	☐	
trust	☐	
warn	☐	
wave	☐	

school

assignment	☐	
bell	☐	
class	☐	
corridor	☐	
gate	☐	
grade	☐	
homework	☐	
report	☐	
rule	☐	
schoolyard	☐	
sign	☐	
stairs	☐	
strict	☐	
uniform	☐	

social media

abuse	☐	
account	☐	
activity	☐	

	New word?	Notes / connected words
bot	☐	
celebrity	☐	
communication	☐	
content	☐	
design	☐	
device	☐	
emoji	☐	
fake	☐	
fame	☐	
filter	☐	
follower	☐	
font	☐	
friend request	☐	
hater	☐	

social media - verbs

block	☐
chat	☐
check	☐
click	☐
comment	☐
delete	☐
edit	☐
like	☐
post	☐
reply	☐
scroll	☐
search	☐
send	☐
surf	☐
tag	☐
track	☐
upload	☐

🌐 Find out more

Find out more

1. Which sites contain more abuse?

Are some social media platforms more popular with bullies than others?
List 5 - 10 different social networks in order of how much bullying or trolling you think they contain.

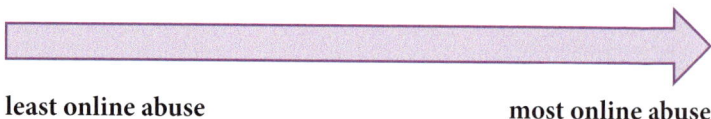

least online abuse   **most online abuse**

2. Fake news

Find an example of fake news which publishes wrong or misleading information.

• Compare it to the correct information: what was changed?

• Why do you think they did this?

3. Hateful content

Find some examples of divisive, hateful posts or comments on social media.
What effect does this have on the reader or viewer?

4. Prevent cyberbullying

What can we do to stop cyberbullying?
Investigate some interesting and effective campaigns to give you some ideas.
List 5 things you can do to help reduce or prevent online abuse for your friends and classmates.

Stop the bullies!

1. _____
   _____

2. _____
   _____

3. _____
   _____

4. _____
   _____

5. _____
   _____

5. Make a poster

Make a poster to help prevent cyberbullying.

Answer key

Focus on the story

Questions at the end of each chapter

Chapter 1
- She has mixed feeling. It means a change to her routine and early starts, but she is quietly optimistic, even a bit excited.
- She'll get to spend every day with Tim and people will be jealous of what a perfect couple they make.

Chapter 2
- She spends hours every day choosing the right photo, editing, deciding on a tag, selecting fonts and designs, and planning the best time of day to post.
- They are a bit jealous.

Chapter 3
- She felt nervous, ugly, and worried. She didn't want to see anyone.
- She's worried about her physical appearance and that people are laughing at her. Not knowing who the troll is, makes her not sure she can trust anyone.

Chapter 4
- She was still thinking about who the troll could be, and she was very worried about how ugly her ears were.
- She was now sure that her ears were so ugly that they had to be hidden.

Chapter 5
- She didn't want to go out and see anybody, even though Tim tried to persuade her.
- She was too stubborn.

Chapter 6
- She liked the fact that people were paying attention to her and showing her respect.
- She feels excited, powerful and a little nervous.

Chapter 7

- She really needed to talk about it as she hadn't yet shared her feelings with anyone about it.
- Carly had a clear motive – she was jealous because Sam was getting so much online time and comments, and people were paying her so much attention.

Chapter 8

- The troll knows that Sam and Tim are together, and they are jealous.
- She tried to argue the case logically. They've been friends for 10 years, Carly like being popular, but she wasn't against Sam being popular too.

Chapter 9

- She started the trolling. She's stopped it now, but she wants to make sure that nobody finds out that it was her.
- She wants to stay away from all the posts and comments, and just keep her head down.

Chapter 10

- Her friends weren't helping and she wasn't ready to tell her parents yet, so she thought it would be useful to talk to somebody from the school.
- If she accepts that it isn't Carly, she will have to start right back from the beginning and look for new suspects.

Chapter 11

- It was the only way she could be sure that she won't experience more troll trouble in the future.
- Very well. Miss Hill had prepared them both well for it, and they had had time to think before they met.

Chapter 12

- She didn't have a chance at popularity and fame.
- It's much easier to type unkind comments than to say them directly to somebody's face.

Focus on the story

1 **1** T, **2** T, **3** F - they send messages in Mr Wilson's science class, **4** F - the school has strict uniform rules, **5** T, **6** T , **7** F - Tim begged Sam to go to Joe Walker's party, she ignored his message so he went to her house to convince her, **8** F - Emma' brother is younger than her; 8 years old, **9** F - Kelly says Sam doesn't deserve this online abuse, **10** F - Emma had an old, abandoned phone in her drawer which she used to create girlzpower, **11** T, **12** F - Tim and Zoe try to convince Sam that Carly isn't the troll; they have been best friends since the first year of primary school, **13** F - Kelly asks Emma why she hasn't been online recently, but she never suspects she is the troll, **14** T, **15** T

2 **1** g, **2** e, **3** j, **4** h, **5** b, **6** f, **7** d, **8** a, **9** c, **10** i

3 **1** the schoolyard, **2** Sam's bedroom, **3** the schoolyard, **4** Sam's bedroom, **5** the schoolyard, **6** the park, **7** Miss Hill's office, **8** Miss Hill's office, **9** the café, **10** the school cafeteria

Focus on the people

1. **1** Carly, **2** Mr Wilson, **3** styloz4real, **4** Sam's mum, **5** Miss Hill, **6** Sam, **7** Tim, **8** Kelly, **9** Zoe, **10** Emma

Focus on grammar

1 anxiety, angry, confident, confusion, doubt, excited, fear, frustration, guilty, happiness, importance, jealousy, alone/lonely, luck, nervous, optimism, paranoia, popularity, power, relieved, sadness, safe, self-conscious, stress, surprise, suspicious, tense, ugliness, vulnerable, worry

2. **1** Why hasn't he dumped you yet? **2** Why would someone say that? **3** Why do they have that rule? **4** What will Tim think of her big ears? **5** Why didn't Carly and Zoe mention her big

ears? **6** What have I done to her? **7** Does everyone think I have witch ears? **8** Why are they doing this to me? **9** Why didn't you tell us by phone? **10** Why couldn't everyone just talk about something else?

3. **1** Sam had blocked, **2** she hadn't shared, **3** Emma had felt, **4** she had failed, **5** It had happened, **6** Emma had decided, **7** she had overreacted, **8** she had done, **9** Emma had already decided

Focus on words

Emma's emotions and feelings: positive emotions - excited, important **negative emotions** - bad, fear, guilty, sad **both positive & negative emotions** - nervous, powerful

Sam's emotions and feelings: positive emotions - confident, excited, happy, lucky, optimistic, pleased, popular, relief, safe **negative emotions** - alone, anger, confused, doubt, fear, frustrated, jealous, paranoid, scared, stressed, suspicious, ugly, upset, vulnerable **both positive & negative emotions** - anxiety, nervous, relaxed, self-conscious, surprised, tense, worried